W9- AUW -O66

This book belongs to:

_____

_____

Keep a light shining
in your window
during the holidays
and a warm feeling
toward others shining
in your heart all year.

HOLIDAY TRADITIONS

by Debbie Mumm

Loving Traditions for the Whole Family

new seasons®

A Christmas Letter
🌿 from Debbie 🌿

Christmas means so many things to me. However, when I sit and think about it, "continuity" is the thought that I keep landing on. With all the changes, stages of life, changes in family, and the evolution of traditions, one thing that has been steadfast in my life is the celebration of Christmas.

My collective holiday memories from childhood are about magic, anticipation, special gifts, family times, baking cookies, singing, how simple my world was, and how happy Christmas made me. The magic of Christmas was overwhelming.

And when I think back about all the stages of my life—becoming an adult and creating Christmas in my own home, becoming a mother and bringing Christmas to my little boy, moving to new towns, having parties for my friends, experiencing the pains of loss of family and the joy of new and deepening friendships— I realize my feelings about Christmas really haven't changed too much.

For me, Christmas has always been about a loving spirit that we share. And, no matter what else is happening in our lives, we celebrate it every year because it fills our hearts with love.

Debbie Mumm

❧ Table of Contents ❧

Timeless Traditions 8

Our Family Traditions 10

Twelve Days of Christmas 12

The Gift of the Magi 14

Children's Gingerbread Party 16

Scenting Your Home 18

The Last Christmas Tree 20

Christmas Greetings 22

When I Was Little 24

Cookie Exchange 26

The Best Christmas Tree Ever 28

Finding Faith 30

Remembering Our Furry and Feathered Friends 32

Caroling and Wassailing 34

The Snow Ball 36

Gifts From the Heart 38

Gift-Wrapping Get-Together 40

Light the Way 42

Christmas Kisses 44

Christmas Eve 46

A Visit From St. Nicholas 48

Stocking Stories 50

Christmas Day 52

Christmas Memories 56

Thank You, Dear 60

Timeless Traditions

I believe traditions are created and adopted to comfort us. Traditions create anticipation and expectations. Traditions at Christmas do create constancy from year to year, however part of the fun is watching them evolve over time as we grow and change.

Our traditions can also be closely related to the region we live in. Living in the great Northwest, I'm still very attached to the idea of having a real Christmas tree. Rather than shopping for a tree at an outdoor lot, I enjoy visiting a tree farm and picking out my own. I make a whole day of it, bringing some friends and family, packing some lunches and hot cocoa, and playing our favorite Christmas carols all the way!

Another fun tradition can be the annual photo with Santa, with a spin: Try including the whole family in the photo, and continue the tradition even after the kids are grown. Think of how hilarious the photo session will be when all the kids are in college! And, the photos will be a cherished keepsake of Christmas through the years.

Traditions shared with friends and family are wonderful, but don't forget to take some time to treat yourself. Here are some of my favorite personal traditions I have come to enjoy over the years. I'm pretty sure you'll also get into the holiday spirit if you give one a try:

❇ Make it a special treat for yourself to have an eggnog or gingerbread latte (my faves) while you're out shopping. Put your feet up and enjoy!

❇ Play Christmas music in your car so you hear it wherever you are. I love Christmas music and have a large collection. From Thanksgiving on, I have it playing at the office, in the car, and at home.

❇ Buy a little gift for someone who isn't expecting it. Sometimes someone you know may need a little lift, and you want them to know how much you appreciate them. To see their face light up will bring you both real joy.

❇ Make your charitable contributions. This can be a family thing or your own private way of giving. I try to do it well in advance of the holidays when it's for a food bank or Christmas fund—so families can get what they need in plenty of time for the holiday.

❇ Set aside an evening to watch your favorite Christmas movie. (Mine is *White Christmas*, but I also love *It's a Wonderful Life* and *Little Women*.) Cuddle under a cozy blanket with your slippers and jammies on—the movie will be even better then!

Our Family Traditions

Every family is different, and a family's traditions are a unique reflection of the love and devotion felt in the home. You can use the opposite page to record some of your own special traditions, which you can look back on in years to come. To get you started, I've included some of my own favorites, which have made my holidays sweet throughout the years:

❉ Let your children choose a special ornament every Christmas. Think how fun it will be to hand your grown children their own personal collection of Christmas ornaments as a starter set for their first Christmas tree.

❉ When your family is young, you can start a tradition of reading your favorite Christmas stories or prayers on Christmas Eve. Read them when you are all gathered together to eat your meal, or before opening presents.

❉ Plan an annual outing to see all the Christmas lights around town. Pack hot chocolate in portable cups and cookies in a basket and have a fun evening oohing and ahhing over the holiday light displays.

When we light our Christmas tree ....

....

....

Our family's Christmas dinner blessing is ....

....

....

For Santa Claus and his reindeer, we ....

....

....

First thing Christmas morning, we ....

....

....

We decorate our home ....

....

....

Our favorite kind of Christmas tree is ....

....

At the tippy-top of our Christmas tree is ....

....

Our oldest ornament is from ....

....

Christmas wouldn't be the same without ....

....

....

TWELVE
DAYS of CHRISTMAS

On the first day of Christmas
my true love sent to me:
A Partridge in a Pear Tree

On the second day of Christmas
my true love sent to me:
Two Turtle Doves
and a Partridge in a Pear Tree

On the third day of Christmas
my true love sent to me:
Three French Hens
Two Turtle Doves
and a Partridge in a Pear Tree

On the fourth day of Christmas
my true love sent to me:
Four Calling Birds
Three French Hens
Two Turtle Doves
and a Partridge in a Pear Tree

On the fifth day of Christmas
my true love sent to me:
Five Golden Rings
Four Calling Birds
Three French Hens
Two Turtle Doves
and a Partridge in a Pear Tree

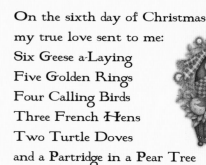

On the sixth day of Christmas
my true love sent to me:
Six Geese a-Laying
Five Golden Rings
Four Calling Birds
Three French Hens
Two Turtle Doves
and a Partridge in a Pear Tree

On the seventh day of Christmas
my true love sent to me:
Seven Swans a-Swimming
Six Geese a-Laying
Five Golden Rings
Four Calling Birds
Three French Hens
Two Turtle Doves
and a Partridge in a Pear Tree

On the eighth day of Christmas
my true love sent to me:
Eight Maids a-Milking
Seven Swans a-Swimming
Six Geese a-Laying
Five Golden Rings
Four Calling Birds
Three French Hens
Two Turtle Doves
and a Partridge in a Pear Tree

On the ninth day of Christmas
my true love sent to me:
Nine Ladies Dancing
Eight Maids a-Milking
Seven Swans a-Swimming
Six Geese a-Laying
Five Golden Rings
Four Calling Birds
Three French Hens
Two Turtle Doves
and a Partridge in a Pear Tree

On the tenth day of Christmas
my true love sent to me:
Ten Lords a-Leaping
Nine Ladies Dancing
Eight Maids a-Milking
Seven Swans a-Swimming
Six Geese a-Laying
Five Golden Rings
Four Calling Birds
Three French Hens
Two Turtle Doves
and a Partridge in a Pear Tree

On the eleventh day of Christmas
my true love sent to me:
Eleven Pipers Piping
Ten Lords a-Leaping
Nine Ladies Dancing
Eight Maids a-Milking
Seven Swans a-Swimming
Six Geese a-Laying
Five Golden Rings
Four Calling Birds
Three French Hens
Two Turtle Doves
and a Partridge in a Pear Tree

On the twelfth day of Christmas
my true love sent to me:
Twelve Drummers Drumming
Eleven Pipers Piping
Ten Lords a-Leaping
Nine Ladies Dancing
Eight Maids a-Milking
Seven Swans a-Swimming
Six Geese a-Laying
Five Golden Rings
Four Calling Birds
Three French Hens
Two Turtle Doves
and a Partridge in a Pear Tree

When we hear this song, most of us just delight in the playful, festive imagery it conjures up. But this song was originally written to help Catholic children secretly learn the tenets of their faith at a time when it was forbidden to practice Catholicism in England.

THE GIFT of the MAGI

Based on the original story by O. Henry

Della had scrimped and saved all year, and all she had to show for it was one dollar and eighty-seven cents. What possible sort of present could she buy for Jim with that? Certainly not one that would be fitting for such a wonderful husband.

Della held the meager amount in her hand. It might as well have been nothing. She sat down on the shabby little couch for a good cry, for there seemed nothing else for her to do.

Presently, Della stopped crying and went to the mirror to repair the evidence of her weeping. She washed her face and reapplied her powder. As she turned from the mirror she saw it. She looked back at the mirror and quickly took her hair down. It hung down almost to her knees, luxurious and shiny and brown.

Della and Jim had just two items of value. One was Della's beautiful hair, befitting a queen. The other was Jim's pocket watch. It was a watch worthy of the finest gentleman. So what could Della be thinking as she gazed at her finest treasure in a small and cracked mirror?

"My hair," Della said sadly as she put it back up. She pulled on her thread-bare coat and hurried through the gray, winter streets until she came to a shop whose sign read, "Madame Sofronie. Hair Goods."

"Will you buy my hair?" Della asked, half hoping the answer would be no.

"I will give you twenty dollars," said Madame Sofronie as Della let her hair cascade down. And so the deed was done.

Della spent the next few hours looking in shops until she found it. It was the perfect watch chain for Jim, simple and handsome in design.

Della hurried home, did what she could to repair the damage of her shorn hair, and put dinner on.

Della heard Jim's footsteps on the stairs. She went pale for a moment thinking of what he'd say when he saw her.

Jim stood frozen in the doorway with the strangest look on his face. Della broke the silence. "Merry Christmas, Jim. I've sold my hair so I could buy you a proper gift. You don't really mind, do you? I had to do it, and my hair grows so very fast, and . . . "

"You've cut your hair?" Jim asked as if he couldn't see that she had. "You say your hair is gone?"

"I've sold it, Jim. I did it because I love you. Shall we have dinner?"

Jim pulled a package out of his pocket and handed it to Della. "Della, there's nothing you could do that would stop me from loving you, but if you open this package I'm sure you'll see why I seemed surprised."

Della quickly tore open the package. Her shout of joy was instantly replaced with tears, for in the package were beautiful, jewel-studded combs she had once seen in a shop window and yearned for ever since. Now these combs were hers, but the beautiful hair they were meant to hold was gone.

Wiping away tears, Della remembered Jim's gift. She handed it to him saying, "Isn't it beautiful? Here, give me your watch. I want to put the chain on it."

Instead of pulling his watch out of his pocket, Jim sat down on the couch with a smile. "Della," he said. "Let's put away our gifts for a while. I sold the watch to get the money to buy the combs. Now, my love, let's have dinner."

Children's Gingerbread Party

Children love to be involved in all things Christmas, and what could be more fun than a gingerbread decorating party? Create some wonderful moments with the special children in your life while adding frosting and candies to sweet treats like gingerbread men and gingerbread houses! Whether made from graham crackers, scratch, or a kit, making a gingerbread house with your kids will hold a special place in both your decorating and your memory. For smaller children, decorate gingerbread men together using frosting, raisins, and hard candies. When all the decorating is done, serve warm spiced cider or hot chocolate and enjoy eating some of your creations.

EASY "GINGERBREAD" HOUSE

Use an empty and rinsed ½ pint cardboard milk or juice container as the base for each gingerbread house. Break graham crackers to fit sides and top of container. Attach graham crackers to container with prepared frosting. Decorate house as desired with colored icings, cereal, pretzels, hard candies, or gum drops.

Hot Buttered Cider

⅓ cup packed brown sugar
¼ cup butter, softened
¼ cup honey
¼ teaspoon ground cinnamon
¼ teaspoon ground nutmeg
3 quarts (12 cups) apple cider or juice

Beat sugar, butter, honey, cinnamon and nutmeg until fluffy. Heat cider until hot. Fill mugs with hot cider; stir in 1 tablespoon butter mixture for each 1 cup cider. Makes 12 servings.

MINTY SWIRL COCOA

3 ounces semisweet chocolate, finely chopped

¼ cup sugar

4 cups milk, divided

1 teaspoon vanilla

Marshmallows and peppermint sticks, to garnish

Combine chocolate, sugar, and ¼ cup milk in medium saucepan over medium heat. Cook, stirring constantly until chocolate melts. Add remaining 3¾ cups milk; heat until hot. Do not boil. Remove from heat; stir in vanilla. Beat with wire whisk until frothy. Pour into mugs and top with marshmallows. Serve with peppermint stick. Makes 8 (½ cup) servings.

Gingerbread Cookies

3½ cups all-purpose flour

2 teaspoons ground cinnamon

1½ teaspoons ground ginger

1 teaspoon salt

1 teaspoon baking soda

1 teaspoon allspice

¼ teaspoon cloves

1 cup butter

2 eggs

1 cup packed brown sugar

⅓ cup dark molasses

1 teaspoon vanilla

Assorted colored frostings, small decors, and colored sugars

Combine flour, cinnamon, ginger, salt, soda, allspice, and cloves in medium bowl; set aside. Beat butter and sugar in large bowl until light and fluffy. Beat in eggs, molasses, and vanilla. Gradually add flour mixture; beat until well blended. Shape dough in 3 discs; cover and refrigerate for at least 2 hours.

Preheat oven to 350°F. Working with 1 portion at a time, roll out dough on lightly floured surface to ¼-inch thickness. Cut out with cookie cutters. Place cookies 1 inch apart on lightly greased cookie sheets. Bake 10 minutes or until firm. Let stand on cookie sheets 1 minute. Remove cookies to wire racks; cool. Decorate as desired. Store in airtight containers. Makes about 3 dozen cookies.

Scenting Your Home

They say that our sense of smell has the longest, strongest memory of all our senses. If you've ever been transported back in time by the smell of white paste, wet wool, or your mother's perfume, you'll agree that the power to hold a time and place in your memory is largely due to how it all smelled!

I find that lightly scenting my home helps to anchor holiday memories in the minds and hearts of my friends and family. Remember that the keys to successful home-scenting are "don't overdo it" and "choose scents from the same family." For instance, a simmering pot on the stove will likely waft through your whole home, so if you also wish to burn candles, burn unscented ones. Candles, on the other hand, are more likely to scent a room or two, so choose families like "greeneries," "sweets," or "herbs and everlastings."

Simmering Pot

Make a festive simmering pot to fill your kitchen with a sweet and spicy citrus scent. To a large pot of water, add the peels of any citrus fruits you have handy. Oranges, tangerines, grapefruit, lemons, and limes all work well. Sprinkle in cinnamon, allspice, and nutmeg, as well as whole cloves and cinnamon sticks, for spicy appeal. Let the pot simmer on low heat, and enjoy the scents!

SCENTED CANDLES

Scenting your own candles isn't time-consuming or complicated, and you can use any unscented pillar candles you have around the house. Heat the tip of a metal skewer over a flame, and use it to poke five or six 1-inch-deep holes around the top of the candle. Pour a few drops of essential oil into each hole. Light and enjoy!

SCENTED PINE CONES

Fill a sealable plastic bag with dry, clean pine cones. Sprinkle a liberal amount of essential oil on a few facial tissues, and add them to the bag of pine cones. Try oil of cinnamon, clove, cedar, or orange. You can use one oil, or combine oils for your own custom scent. Seal the bag and let it sit for several days. Check the bag every few days until you are happy with the strength of the scent. Place the pine cones in your rooms to add the warmth of fragrance to your home!

Homemade Potpourri

Common herbs and spices, some of which you may already have, can make an aromatic and beautiful decoration for your home. To make a good base for your potpourri, use the leaves and flowers of rosemary, lavender, mint, chamomile, and sage. Add cinnamon sticks, whole cloves, and a few drops of essential oil to make a long-lasting scent. Put all the ingredients in a festive ceramic bowl, and display it in the room of your choice.

THE LAST CHRISTMAS TREE

For my family, the busiest time of the year is between Thanksgiving and Christmas. That's because we're in the Christmas tree business. Just when most people are taking time off to be with their families or do their Christmas shopping, we're busy cutting and selling Christmas trees. The hard work is over as soon as we sell our last tree. Then it's time to decorate our own tree and enjoy Christmas.

One particular Christmas Eve started out like all the others, but it ended up being my favorite one ever. It happened when I was ten years old, but to me it seems like only yesterday . . .

❄ ❄ ❄ ❄ ❄

"I'm sure glad it's finally Christmas Eve," says Grandpa as he ties a Christmas tree to the roof of a car. Mom, Dad, my sister Anne, and I (I'm Owen) are all busy with our jobs. We nod in agreement. Mom notices that the best trees are almost gone. "Pop, make sure you put one aside for us," she says. Grandpa picks a tall fir and puts it away in the barn.

Soon Dad sells the last tree. I'm sent down to the road to put up the "Sold Out" sign. A car pulls in. I chase it back up the road, but by the time I get to the front yard a man and two kids have already gotten out of the car.

"You sure you don't have any trees left, not even a little one?" the man asks.

"How come you waited till now to shop for a tree?" I ask.

"Owen, shush!" scolds Anne.

One of the children, a little girl, pipes up. "We've been at the hospital with Mama. She's sick. But they're letting her go home tomorrow. We're going to give her the best Christmas."

The man put his arm around the girl. "Well, I guess we'll be going," he says.

"Hang on a second," says Grandpa as he motions for Dad to come with him. A moment later the two of them come out of the barn with the tree that had been set aside. "I almost forgot about this one. Owen, run and get the twine." I do as I'm told even though I know that we're about to lose our Christmas tree.

Dad, Grandpa, and the man tie the tree to the car. The man reaches for his wallet, but Grandpa won't take any money. "Merry Christmas!" Grandpa says cheerfully.

"Let me pay you," says the man.

"Once my Grandpa's made a decision, there's no changing his mind," I tell the man.

The man looks embarrassed, or maybe it's the cold that makes his face red. "Thank you very much," he says.

After the man and his children drive off, we go into the house. Exhausted, we all sit down with a sigh, all except me. I spot the boxes of Christmas tree decorations sitting in the corner. I pull out the decorations. I wrap a shiny garland around myself and hang an ornament from a lampshade. What next? I string lights around the hat rack and plug them in. Anne joins in. Mom laughs at her Christmas-decorated kids and makes hot cocoa and sandwiches.

Soon Grandpa and Dad are decorating the walls and the furniture. I hang an ornament from our dog's collar. Finally, I climb on the back of a chair to put the angel on top of the hat rack. I throw my arms open and shout, "Merry Christmas!" And it is.

Christmas Greetings

Sending Christmas cards has been a long-standing tradition in our culture. It is a wonderful way to stay in touch with friends and family who aren't part of daily life or whom we don't see over the holiday season. Even though it's not our intention, it can be difficult to keep in touch with those far away. This annual greeting can keep your connection in place. Photos are also incredible to receive every year—they tell you so much. But what they don't tell, you can include in a letter. However you communicate, it is your personal touch that will be most appreciated.

If you can't find the time to make your own cards, try embellishing some simple store-bought cards with ribbon, buttons, stickers, glitter, and whatever crafty odds and ends you may have lying around.

Or, for an extra-personal touch, make photo-frame cards out of recent family photos. Fold over a piece of good quality paper, attach the photo on the center of the front with double-stick tape or photo-friendly glue, and glue a pretty ribbon around the edges for a border. Let it dry, then write your greeting on the inside. While you're at it, you can even think ahead and create some thank-you cards that coordinate with your Christmas cards!

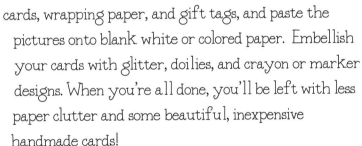

Recycle as much as possible to avoid creating unnecessary waste. One way to do this is to collage new greeting cards out of cut-up paper scraps from previous Christmases. The kids can make cards for their friends while you make cards for yours. Cut up old cards, wrapping paper, and gift tags, and paste the pictures onto blank white or colored paper. Embellish your cards with glitter, doilies, and crayon or marker designs. When you're all done, you'll be left with less paper clutter and some beautiful, inexpensive handmade cards!

When it comes to displaying those cards you receive, make sure to put them in a place where all can enjoy: the mantelpiece (with care!), strung in the main hallway, or around the kitchen windowsills. For a homey touch, try using a long ribbon to hang them on, using clothes pins or paper clips to keep them in place. They'll remind you of your nearest and dearest, and they will warm your heart whenever you see them.

When I Was Little

For an extra-special family keepsake, ask older family members or friends to write—or dictate to you—about Christmases when they were little children.

My Favorite Christmas Memories
By_____

_____

_____

_____

_____

_____

My Favorite Christmas Memories
By_____

_____

_____

_____

_____

_____

My Favorite Christmas Memories

By_____

_____

_____

_____

_____

_____

_____

My Favorite Christmas Memories

By_____

_____

_____

_____

_____

_____

_____

My Favorite Christmas Memories

By_____

_____

_____

_____

_____

_____

_____

Cookie  Exchange

I have a friend who takes a week off work just to bake Christmas cookies! While she does have dozens and dozens of different cookies to serve and enjoy throughout the season, I can think of a few better ways to spend a week off than in my kitchen covered in flour! That's why I like to host or attend a cookie exchange every year. I bring one huge batch of cookies and leave with a selection that rivals my cookie-baking friend's.

The rules for a cookie exchange are simple. In the invitation, set the number of cookies each person should bring. Remind people that the boxes they bring will also serve to carry home the cookies they receive. And finally, ask people to print out enough recipe cards for the whole group.

When I host a cookie party, I like to serve savories (this pimiento one does the trick) and veggies to "cut" the sugary treats we're sure to taste-test. To give your home a scent to complement the just-baked aroma of the cookies, hang orange and clove pomanders throughout the house.

QUICK PIMIENTO CHEESE SNACKS

❧

2 ounces cream cheese, softened
½ cup (2 ounces) shredded Cheddar cheese
1 jar (2 ounces) diced pimiento, drained
2 tablespoons finely chopped pecans
½ teaspoon hot pepper sauce
24 French bread slices, ¼-inch thick,
or party bread slices

❧

Preheat broiler. Mix together cheeses. Stir in pimiento, pecans, and pepper sauce. Place bread slices on nonstick baking sheet. Broil 4 inches from heat until lightly toasted on both sides. Spread cheese mixture onto bread slices. Broil 1 to 2 minutes or until topping is hot and bubbly. Serve immediately. Makes 24 servings.

Cookie Notes

❧

_____
_____
_____
_____
_____
_____
_____
_____
_____
_____
_____
_____
_____
_____

ORANGE AND CLOVE POMANDERS

❧

These easy-to-make pomanders will add a beautiful and traditional touch to your Christmas decor. Use the pointed end of a toothpick to poke small holes all around an orange, leaving about ¼ inch between holes (make just a few holes at first and stick cloves into holes to determine the distance between the holes). When all the holes have been made, stick the whole cloves in the holes. Cover the entire surface of the orange. Tie pretty ribbon around the orange, making a loop for hanging if you want to display the pomander on your tree. You can also wrap ribbon around the pomanders for a decorative touch. Stack a few oranges in a bowl or use them to accent your mantel arrangement. They will add homemade beauty as well as Christmasy fragrance to your home.

The Best Christmas Tree Ever

E very Christmas season, I feel like that year's tree is the best one ever. So I asked a few friends if they had stories of memorable Christmas trees. Here are some of the memories they shared with me.

❋ "When we were first married, we didn't have many ornaments, so we decorated the tree with bright, shiny fishing lures, particularly those that were handed down from my husband's grandfather. To this day, we make sure we have a lure or other fish-related ornaments on our tree."

❋ "When I was single, my roommate and I had no Christmas ornaments and no family close by. So to make our apartment festive we had a tree-decorating party. We made sugar cookies, using a straw to make a hole near the top of each one. Our guests decorated the cookie ornaments with colorful homemade frosting, strung popcorn and cranberries, and tied velvet bows for the tree. It was a great time to share Christmas memories and enjoy each person's creativity."

❋ "One year my three adult children surprised me with a decorated tree. We own a tree farm, so the three snuck out in the middle of the night, chopped down a tree I had marked, and had it up and decorated before daylight. Needless to say, I was delighted!"

THE HISTORY OF CHRISTMAS TREES

For thousands of years, the Egyptian, Roman, and Druid cultures, among others, worshipped the evergreen tree as a symbol of eternal life and the coming of spring. In the Middle Ages, Germans and Scandinavians began to adopt the tradition, eventually decorating evergreen trees with lights and ornaments as a symbol of Christmas. Since then, evergreen trees have become a lasting image of Christmas warmth and spirit, delighting us with their wonderful pine scent and simple beauty.

Cinnamon Ornaments

This fun and simple craft will add a wonderful cinnamon scent to your tree. Mix 1 cup ground cinnamon and ¾ cup applesauce to form a stiff dough. Add additional applesauce 1 tablespoon at a time, if needed to form dough. Roll out to ¼-inch thickness. Cut out with cookie cutters. Make small hole, with small straw or large toothpick, in each ornament for ribbon hangers. Let air dry about one week, turning over occasionally, or bake at 200°F, 1½ hours. Decorate with fabric paints if you like. Makes 6 to 8 ornaments. Note: It's probably best to use these only for one year.

A Northwest Christmas

Every culture, every community, and even every family decorates its trees in unique ways that say something about their own traditions. In the Northwest, it is customary to feature forest animals, fish, and sports equipment on Christmas trees. I have a friend whose husband gives her a different themed ornament every year—last year it was a kayak! I think it's neat to start your own tree-decorating tradition, based on your local culture or personal interests. After a few years, you'll have created a keepsake collection of special ornaments you can enjoy and add to.

Finding Faith

What Grace wanted more than anything in the whole world for Christmas was a kitten. She didn't care if it was snow white or orange striped. She didn't care if it had green eyes or yellow eyes. She only cared if it was truly her kitten.

Grace should have known better than to hope for a kitten. Mama and Papa had both been out of work, and Grace knew that all she could hope for this Christmas was something she really needed, like socks. She would not be getting something she really wanted, like a furry kitten that would lick her nose with a sandpaper tongue and follow a piece of yarn she dragged behind her. She knew better than to hope. But still, she did just that: hoped.

The town was busy with Christmas: Christmas shopping, Christmas baking, and Christmas decorating. Grace wasn't interested in the shopping. She had no money to buy gifts. She also had no interest in the baking. To watch the shelves in the bakery fill up with Christmas cookies frosted and speckled with sugar only made her tummy complain.

Now, decorating was another thing. Grace liked watching the men on ladders stringing lights. She liked standing in front of a store window as they frosted the glass inside with "snow."

But most of all she liked to watch them set up the crèche in front of the church.

First they built a miniature stable. They hammered and nailed, and one of the men let Grace hammer a nail. They filled the stable with straw that smelled good and clean. Next they carried out the figures for the crèche. Each one was carefully unwrapped and placed in its proper place. Grace watched the empty stable fill, and it was like the figures came to life. Every day after that, Grace visited the crèche.

On Christmas Eve Grace stood under a dark and cloudy sky in front of the crèche and prayed one more time for a kitten. Just then the clouds burst open and snow fell in huge, icy flakes. Grace tried to make her way home, but the pieces of snow and ice stung her face and the wind jostled her. She went back to the crèche and crept inside the stable. It wasn't so bad once she got out of the wind and snow.

In the darkness of the stable, Grace heard a tiny "Mew, mew." First Grace spotted two round, green eyes and then two white spots. As Grace's eyes got used to the dark she saw that it was a coal-black kitten with two white-tipped feet. "Mew," said the kitten as it snuggled against Grace. 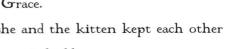 Grace lifted the kitten gently into her coat, and she and the kitten kept each other warm until the blizzard blew past, just as suddenly as it had begun.

Grace, with the kitten still tucked all warm and safe in her coat, crawled out of the stable onto the fresh, glistening snow. In the distance Grace spotted her parents. She ran to them.

"Bless you, you're safe!" cried Grace's mother, pulling her into a tight, warm hug.

"We're safe," said Grace as she showed her parents the kitten. "I'm naming her Faith," Grace told them, "because I had faith that I would get a kitten."

"That's a perfect name," said Mama. "Because during the blizzard, when we couldn't find you, we had faith that we would. And here you are!"

With Faith tucked snuggly in her coat, and each mittened hand holding tightly onto a parent's hand, Grace headed home with her family and her new friend.

Remembering Our Furry and Feathered Friends

©Debbie Mumm

All year round, our pets give us their loyalty and love, without asking for too much in return. The holidays are a perfect time to reward them with some treats to show our appreciation. They may not be able to tell you with words, but you'll probably guess by the wagging tail, humming purr, and cheerful chirps that your efforts are very much appreciated! Kids will also love to get involved in the baking and making of treats for their furry and feathered friends.

Peanutty Doggie Treats

❧

2½ cups flour

½ cup oatmeal

1¼ Tbsp. baking powder

1¼ cups peanut butter

1 cup milk

❧

Preheat oven to 400°F. Cover cookie sheet with foil. Combine flour, oatmeal, and baking powder in a large bowl. Add peanut butter and milk; stir until thoroughly mixed. Knead dough; roll out dough on floured surface to ¼-inch thickness. Cut out with cookie cutters. Place on prepared cookie sheets. Bake 20 minutes or until lightly brown. Cool completely on foil.

KITTY KOOKIES

❧

1¼ cups flour

⅓ cup powdered milk

2 teaspoons catnip

⅓ cup milk

1 egg

2 tablespoons vegetable oil

1 tablespoon molasses

❧

Preheat oven to 350°F. Combine flour, dried milk, and catnip in medium bowl. Add milk, egg, oil, and molasses; mix well. Roll out dough on floured surface to ¼-inch thickness. Using knife, cut ½-inch strips. Cut again into ½-inch strips on the diagonal to make small diamond-shaped pieces. Place on greased cookie sheet. Bake 15 minutes or until light brown. Cool; store in tightly sealed container.

Pinecones "for the Birds"

❧

Cut a 12-inch piece of wire and twist around top (thick) part of pinecone. Repeat with all pinecones. Spread peanut butter onto each pinecone to cover completely. Roll cones in bird seed, pressing seed firmly into cones. Wrap pinecones with plastic wrap and close with decorative ribbon.

Caroling and Wassailing

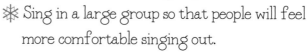

Singing and playing carols is one of my favorite
Christmas traditions. I'm not the greatest singer, but I do
love to sing. And because I can strum a guitar and stumble my
way through on the piano, I've been part of many sing-alongs
throughout the years. One thing I've found is that many people are shy about
singing because they don't do it very often. Because singing is fun and joyful to do as a
group, here are a few ideas for making it fun for even the slightly intimidated.

❄ Sing in a large group so that people will feel
more comfortable singing out.

❄ Have a leader who is comfortable with singing
and who will pick out songs.

❄ Choose simple and well-known songs.

❄ Make a copy of the words for everyone.
Then, sing and repeat only the first couple
verses. Everyone seems to know these best
and won't have to bury their heads trying to
read the words for the lesser-known verses.

❄ An instrument like a guitar or piano will
strengthen your sound and help everyone
follow the tune.

Here we come a-wassailing among the leaves so green...

In Anglo-Saxon times, people would greet each other with the phrase "Waes Hal!" which literally meant "Be Healthy." The tradition of wassailing dates back to the 16th century when young men would gather to sing blessings to their orchards in order to ensure a good yield the following year.

Wassail

2 quarts apple cider

2 cups orange juice

½ cup lemon juice

4 cinnamon sticks

1 teaspoon whole allspice

1 teaspoon whole cloves

1 cup water

¼ cup honey

Combine all ingredients in large saucepan over medium heat. Bring to boil; reduce heat and simmer 30 minutes. Remove spices before serving. Serve hot, from saucepan, garnishing with lemon and orange slices for a festive touch. Makes 12 servings.

SAVORY SAUSAGE CRESCENTS

½ pound sausage

½ cup chopped onion

1 clove garlic, minced

¾ cup shredded Cheddar cheese

¼ teaspoon red pepper flakes

1 package (15 ounces) refrigerated pie crusts (2 crusts)

Brown sausage, onion, and garlic in large nonstick skillet over medium-high heat, stirring to break up meat. Remove from heat; drain off drippings. Stir in cheese and pepper flakes; set aside. Preheat oven to 375°F. Lightly grease cookie sheets. On lightly floured surface, roll 1 pie crust to 14-inch diameter. Cut out circles with 3-inch round cookie cutter. Repeat with second crust, rerolling dough if necessary. Place 1 teaspoon mixture in center of circle; fold dough over filling to form half circle. Moisten edges of dough with water; press together to seal. Repeat with remaining circles. Place on prepared cookie sheets. Bake 12 to 15 minutes or until golden brown. Serve warm. Makes about 2½ dozen crescents. Variation: Use ½ pound ground turkey, ¾ teaspoon poultry seasoning, and ¼ teaspoon salt in place of sausage.

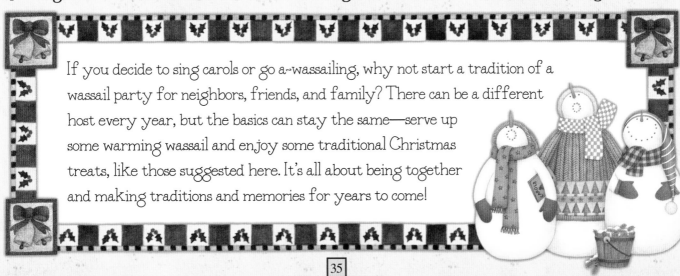

If you decide to sing carols or go a-wassailing, why not start a tradition of a wassail party for neighbors, friends, and family? There can be a different host every year, but the basics can stay the same—serve up some warming wassail and enjoy some traditional Christmas treats, like those suggested here. It's all about being together and making traditions and memories for years to come!

THE SNOW BALL

Legend tells us that on the first night of winter all the snowmen, snowwomen, and snowchildren of the world come together for their celebration of winter. This sparkling celebration is known as the Snow Ball. On this one special night snowpeople can fly, and fly they do to the North Pole, where they attend the ball that celebrates all that is winter. I'm here to tell you this is one legend that is true and to share with you the story of one wonderful Snow Ball that enchanted a most delightful little snowgirl named Wyn.

"Stand still, Wyn!" says Mother as she puts a new jacket around Wyn's shoulders. This jacket isn't plain like her everyday jacket. This jacket is beautiful blue velvet, embroidered with shiny white snowflakes. Then Mother gives Wyn a new hat, not plain like her everyday hat but a fancy hat like the big girls wear. Soon the whole family looks their best. Then comes the wait.

"Why must we wait?" asks Wyn, who thinks she'll melt if she has to wait one minute longer.

"We must wait until exactly midnight. That's when we'll be able to take off," explains Father. If truth be told, Father is ready to burst with excitement, himself.

Suddenly Father, then Mother, then Wyn's brother Cole, then Wyn lift slightly off the snowy ground. "It's time," says Mother. "Stay close."

Wyn has never lifted off the ground. She's not so sure she likes it. "I'm scared," she whispers. But just as quickly, she's up in the dark blue sky whizzing by stars and planets.

Wyn tries to laugh with the joy she's feeling, but she's going too fast. Then . . . whoosh . . . and they've landed.

"Wow!" is all that Wyn can say as she gazes up at the most beautiful blue sky dotted with perfectly shaped stars. The stars seem to be smiling right at Wyn. On the ground are tables and tables covered with food and drink. There's frozen hot chocolate that's hot and cold all at the same time and cakes that are made of sweet snow that disappear in your mouth the moment you taste them. There are strings of colored lights that are made of candy, and when you eat the crackly, sugary treats they glow for a moment in your tummy.

Wyn sees snowchildren from all over the world. "Come play," a little snowgirl shouts, motioning to Wyn.

The snowchildren play in the soft snow. They skate on ice that cushions you when you fall, and they have a snowball fight with snow that tickles when it hits you, even in the face.

The snowchildren sneak back to see what the snowparents are doing, and soon they are joining in on the dance floor, twirling and dancing.

Just as Wyn is starting to feel sleepy, the stars begin dropping from the sky. The snowchildren run through the snow picking up stars to take home.

"When the stars fall, the ball is over," says Father. Snowpeople all around are lifting off the ground. And then Wyn's family is lifting off and zooming through the sky once more.

Soon they are back home. Wyn is sad that the ball is over, but every time she looks at the star she brought back she's reminded of the wonderful time she had, and that soon there will be another Snow Ball.

Gifts from the Heart

Sometimes the most generous gift of all is the gift of your time. This is especially true around the holidays, when much of your time is spoken for. A special hand-written letter to a grandparent, or taking time to take an elderly neighbor on errands or Christmas shopping, is the type of gift that will mean so much to someone special in your life. I have an incredible staff that supports me all year long. The last couple of years I've made each one something special for Christmas. They know better than anyone how busy I am. Their gratitude for the time that I devote to their gifts is the most wonderful gift I could ever receive.

One of my favorite things is to make simple, yet thoughtful gifts that can be treasured throughout the holiday season. These ideas are sure to bring smiles to the lucky recipients!

TWINKLE TOES

A very simple yet special gift can be a pair of festive socks that you embellish yourself. You'll need: purchased socks, lace, beads, jingle bells, buttons, ribbon, needle, and thread. These are perfect as stocking-stuffers, or as an accompaniment to another gift.

HOW-TO: Turn cuff down and hand-sew narrow cotton lace edging to edge of ribbing, stretching out the ribbing as you stitch. When you let go, the lace ruffles automatically. Add small jingle bells. Add wide lace trim to top edge of cotton socks and embellish with beads. Sew buttons and bows to each sock in pairs.

Filled Festive Jars

This one couldn't be easier! Just find some empty jars of any size and decorate them with holiday-themed stickers or punch-outs. Get creative and fill them with your own hot cocoa mix, holiday candy, or even candles. If the jar is missing a lid or you'd like to make one yourself, choose a pretty circle of fabric and secure it with a dainty ribbon in a bow.

The Gift of Yourself

Offering the gift of your time and efforts to someone who needs it is priceless. Here are some ways to make someone's holiday merry without joining the Christmas shopping circus:

❊ Promise to write a letter every month to an elderly relative—it will make their day!

❊ Offer to babysit for a friend on a couple of occasions.

❊ Make homemade I.O.U. certificates promising a free back rub, home-cooked meal, trip to the movies, etc.

❊ Or for kids to parents: I.O.U. certificates for doing the dishes, shoveling the snow, walking the dog, etc.

❊ Volunteer for your favorite organization.

❊ Offer to help someone plant a garden in the spring.

❊ Help a friend organize or paint a room.

❊ Make a huge pot of homemade soup and bring some to the neighbors.

❊ Take your kids and their friends on a mini-field trip to a favorite museum.

Gift-Wrapping Get-Together

One of my co-workers told me about how she makes a wonderful occasion out of gift-wrapping. Each year she and a girlfriend get together before the holidays for a gift-wrapping extravaganza. They share stories, tea, and conversation as they tackle the task of wrapping a mound of presents. Part of the fun is sharing wrapping paper and ribbons to get a wider variety of options, as well as inspiring each other to come up with new festive flourishes or unique ways to wrap oddly-shaped packages. Once wrapped, decorating your packages can be as simple as using ribbon to attach a pine cone or holly branch (try the craft store for more ideas), or using colorful yarn and pretty buttons to embellish the package. Try being earth-friendly by using last year's Christmas cards as recycled gift tags—just cut out a pretty design and punch a hole at the top, securing it to the gift with ribbon. At the end of the evening all the presents are beautifully wrapped, and you've had the enjoyment of each other's company. Sharing the task can turn a chore into a fun occasion.

Mulled Cranberry Tea

2 regular tea bags
1 cup boiling water
1 bottle (48 ounces) cranberry juice
⅓ cup sugar
1 large lemon, thinly sliced
4 cinnamon sticks
6 whole cloves
½ cup dried cranberries

Place tea bags in large pan. Pour boiling water over tea bags; cover and let stand 5 minutes. Discard tea bags. Stir in remaining ingredients. Cover; cook 30 minutes over low heat. Remove and discard lemon slices, cinnamon, and cloves. Serve in warm mugs with additional lemon slice and cinnamon stick.
Makes 8 servings.

WRAPPING TIPS

❄ Choose a theme and wrap the gift accordingly. Use a basket for culinary gifts, a flower pot for gardening supplies, or a pretty towel for bath products.

❄ Shop at an office supply store for inexpensive colored labels and traditional price tags—these can be an innovative alternative to store-bought gift tags.

❄ For a playful gag, wrap a special small present in a small box within a bigger box.

The Perfect Present

The presentation of a gift can be just as important as the gift itself. Think back to the best gifts you've ever received—chances are they were as thoughtfully wrapped as they were chosen. A sprinkle of creativity and some of these materials below are sure to impress and delight the folks on your list.

To tie and embellish:
ribbon
feathers
household string
jute
twine
silk flowers
raffia
plastic beads

To wrap:
colored cellophane
newspaper comics
brown paper bags
mesh
tissue paper
burlap
lace
cheesecloth

Light the Way

The rising of the sun
And the running of the deer,
The playing of the merry organ,
Sweet singing in the choir.

"THE HOLLY AND THE IVY,"
A TRADITIONAL ENGLISH CAROL

Evergreen boughs, candles in windows, grand holiday feasts, and the giving of gifts all harken back to ancient times when people of diverse cultures celebrated the return of the sun after the longest night of the year—winter solstice. By honoring the sun, people believed that its powerful rays would return more quickly, bringing them bountiful harvests once again. Each culture celebrated in unique ways, and many old traditions still exist in some form today. In Mexico, it is traditional to make luminarias, or paper lanterns, and place them along your path to welcome people. I've included this craft here because it's a simple yet beautiful way to welcome guests and carolers.

LUMINARIAS

Gather craft paper lunch bags, a pencil, a hole punch, sand, and votive candles. On one side of the paper bag, stencil in a simple design of your choice. Then punch it out with the hole-punch. Fill the bags with two to three inches of sand and place a candle

securely in the center. Light the candle (this step is reserved for Mom or Dad if the kids are helping out) and place along the path to your front door, or on the front or back porch.

Find out when winter solstice occurs in
your time zone, and celebrate the season!

ICE CANDLES

If you live in a very cold climate, try making these extra-cool candleholders. You'll need medium-size balloons, tea candles, and tap water. Fill balloons about half full of water and knot ends. Set balloons outdoors until you can feel they've frozen solid. Ideally, the middle hasn't yet frozen, though, so keep checking throughout the day. When the water in the balloons is perfectly frozen, pop the balloons and peel away the skins. Discard the rubber pieces with care. Empty any water from inside. Place a tea candle in the center, and arrange these beautiful ice globes around your yard as you wish. Magical!

Christmas Kisses

When my friend Sophie was a little girl, she spent a great deal of time edging her way through doorways, to avoid being caught and smooched under the Christmas mistletoe by her cheek-pinching aunts and uncles. Then one year, when her cousin brought his best friend home for a holiday gathering, she found herself lingering under the mistletoe, clearly hoping for that special holiday kiss! She got her kiss all right, but it was a big noisy smooch on the cheek from her cousin, who knew her scheme exactly!

Back then, Sophie's uncles used to walk far back into the woods to shoot mistletoe from high in the trees, where it grows as a parasite. I'm not about to do that, and I bet you aren't either, so let's assume you're using the artificial variety of mistletoe in your home. Also, as romantic as it is, mistletoe is poisonous, so I do not recommend having it hanging around in homes with small children or pets.

This is the season of opening hearts
and opening our home to one and all;
So let's gather our family, let's welcome our friends,
and greet beneath this kissing ball.

A kissing ball is a pretty alternative to a simple sprig of mistletoe. Using craft glue, adhere small clusters of leaves and berries to a foam ball (try lavender, hollyberries, or cranberries). Make sure to cover any open spaces with a dab of glue and then material. Let the ball dry. Lay out a long ribbon piece, place the ball on top, gather the ribbon over the ball, and tie securely. Do the same thing with another ribbon, "cutting" the ball the other way so that it is in quarters. Take the loose ribbon and tie all four pieces together for hanging. Hang your kissing ball from a doorway or ceiling fixture. If you'd like to make a ball that will last from year to year, try using pretty buttons or beads instead!

The History of Mistletoe

Early Europeans considered mistletoe to be one of the most mysterious, magical, and sacred plants, despite its toxic qualities. Thought to be an aphrodisiac and to bestow life and fertility, it was used in marriage ceremonies, solstice celebrations, and in patching up conflicts between husband and wife. In English history, mistletoe was first used at Christmas in the form of a kissing ball (see craft above) in the 18th century. Mistletoe berries were attached to a ball and hung from the ceiling. It was thought that lovers who kissed beneath this ball would be sure to marry and have a long and happy life together. On the other hand, if a girl underneath the kissing ball remained unkissed, it was thought she would not marry in the following year. Today, mistletoe still symbolizes the warmth and romance of the holidays, and people still use it as an excuse to smooch at Christmastime!

Christmas Eve

When I was a little girl, my family (which was my mom, my dad, and my sister, Julie) opened our packages on Christmas Eve. So that we were able to stay up late that evening, my sister and I took afternoon naps. Santa always made his stop at our house during our naps. Although it was hard for us to fall asleep knowing that Santa was on his way, the anticipation of staying up late to open our gifts was enough incentive to try our best. My sister, who was a couple years younger than me, would have an easier time falling asleep. So when she awoke, I would ask her if she had heard the reindeer hooves and jingle bells on our roof, to which she'd reply, "Yes, I did!" I think that sharing that experience together doubled the joy for us both. Having this tradition to look back on reminds me of the magic and gift of Santa, and how his legend helps the spirit of Christmas stay in our hearts all year round.

Here are some simple ways to help make your family's
Christmas Eve calm and bright:

❋ Include a family gift blessing for the supper table.

❋ Prepare and serve a meal made of simple appetizers and soup.

❋ Deliver a plate of cookies to the neighbors.

❋ Attend a Christmas Eve candlelight service.

❋ Play games — like dominoes or cards.

❋ Take a late-night walk to look for Santa's sleigh
(and to wear out the children).

❋ Serve up a pot of sweet and soothing kettle tea
(warm milk and honey).

FESTIVE MINCEMEAT TARTS

1 package (15 ounces) refrigerated pie crusts (2 crusts)

1½ cups prepared mincemeat

½ cup tart apple, peeled and chopped

⅓ cup golden raisins

⅓ cup chopped walnuts

3 tablespoons frozen apple juice concentrate, thawed

1 tablespoon grated lemon peel

Preheat oven to 400°F. Let pie crust stand at room temperature 20 minutes.
Roll one crust on lightly floured surface to form 13-inch circle. With
cookie-cutters, cut six 4-inch rounds. Fit each pastry round into 2¾-inch muffin cup.
Repeat with remaining crust. Prick inside of crust with fork; bake 8 minutes.

Meanwhile, thoroughly combine remaining ingredients. Fill each crust with
rounded tablespoonful of mincemeat mixture. Press lightly into crust.
Bake 18 to 20 minutes or until crust edges are golden. Cool in pan 5 minutes.

Carefully remove to wire rack. Makes 12 tarts.

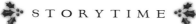
A VISIT FROM ST. NICHOLAS

By Clement C. Moore

'Twas the night before Christmas, when all through the house
Not a creature was stirring, not even a mouse;
The stockings were hung by the chimney with care;
In hopes that St. Nicholas soon would be there;

The children were nestled all snug in their beds,
While visions of sugar-plums danced in their heads;
And Mamma in her 'kerchief, and I in my cap,
Had just settled down for a long winter's nap,

When out on the lawn there arose such a clatter,
I sprang from the bed to see what was the matter.
Away to the window I flew like a flash,
Tore open the shutters and threw up the sash.
The moon on the breast of the new-fallen snow,
Gave the luster of mid-day to objects below,

When, what to my wondering eyes should appear,
But a miniature sleigh, and eight tiny reindeer,
With a little old driver, so lively and quick,
I knew in a moment it must be St. Nick.

More rapid than eagles his coursers they came,
And he whistled, and shouted, and called them by name;
"Now, Dasher! now, Dancer! now, Prancer and Vixen!
On, Comet! On Cupid! on, Donder and Blitzen!
To the top of the porch! to the top of the wall!
Now dash away! dash away! dash away all!"

As dry leaves that before the wild hurricane fly,
If they meet with an obstacle, mount to the sky;
So up to the house-top the coursers they flew,

With the sleigh full of toys, and St. Nicholas too.
And then, in a twinkling, I heard on the roof
The pawing and prancing of each little hoof—

As I drew in my head, and was turning around,
Down the chimney St. Nicholas came with a bound.
He was dressed all in fur, from his head to his foot,
And his clothes were all tarnished with ashes and soot;
A bundle of toys he had flung on his back,
And he looked like a peddler just opening his pack.

His eyes–how they twinkled! His dimples how merry!
His cheeks were like roses, his nose like a cherry!
His droll little mouth was drawn up like a bow,
And the beard on his chin was as white as the snow;
The stump of a pipe he held tight in his teeth,
And the smoke it encircled his head like a wreath;
He had a broad face and a little round belly
That shook, when he laughed, like a bowlful of jelly.

He was chubby and plump, a right jolly old elf;
And I laughed when I saw him, in spite of myself;
A wink of his eye and a twist of his head,
Soon gave me to know I had nothing to dread;
He spoke not a word, but went straight to his work,
And fill'd all the stockings; then turned with a jerk,
And laying his finger aside of his nose,
And giving a nod, up the chimney he rose;

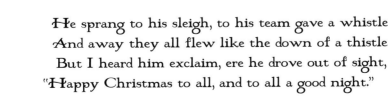

He sprang to his sleigh, to his team gave a whistle,
And away they all flew like the down of a thistle.
But I heard him exclaim, ere he drove out of sight,
"Happy Christmas to all, and to all a good night."

Stocking Stories

It always seems to be the little things that make my Christmas extra bright and magical. That's probably why I get such a kick out of finding the perfect little trinkets to fill the stockings of my loved ones. It's these little personal presents that can sometimes be the most meaningful and special both to give and receive. While you probably already have an idea of what your family will enjoy, I've provided you with a list of my favorites for a little inspiration!

Here are some of the most heart-warming "stocking stories" I've heard from friends over the years:

❄ "When I was little, we lived in an apartment that had no fireplace. My brother and I were afraid that if we didn't have a chimney, Santa wouldn't come. Mother

told us not to worry. She said if Santa couldn't find a chimney, he'd come through the heat vents. So she hung our stockings on the radiator. That Christmas Eve I lay awake, listening. I didn't hear Santa's boots, but the radiator did seem to clunk and hiss more than usual. Santa must've made it through the heat vents, because the next morning when my brother and I ran into the living room, we found our stockings bursting with candy and gifts."

❄ "One year, just before Christmas, I had to have surgery on my ankle. On Christmas Eve, my family decorated my hospital room with tinsel, holly, and a small tree. My favorite decoration, though, was the Christmas stocking. They had glued strips of white cloth around an old sock to make it look like a leg cast. I kept that stocking, and every year I hang it on our mantel to remind me of the year our potentially worst Christmas became our best Christmas."

❄ "The first year my husband and I were married, we couldn't afford Christmas gifts, so we filled each other's stockings with notes describing things we loved about being married. We spent Christmas morning reading about how much we meant to each other. Now we can afford to buy presents, but our favorite gifts are the little love notes we still tuck into each other's stockings."

Little Ideas for Stocking Stuffers

miniature books
sticky notepads
key chain
deck of cards
picture frame
notepad
pin cushion
calendar
travel sewing kit
favorite tea bags
little soaps and lotions
gift certificates
pack of pens or pencils
pack of thank-you notes
pre-paid calling cards
tangerines

The Stocking Tradition

Ever wonder why we hang stockings at Christmas? The origin of this custom dates back hundreds of years to the story of St. Nicholas. In the town of Myra (now in Turkey) there lived a bishop with three daughters. Funds were short at this time, and the nobleman could not afford dowries (money traditionally given to the groom from the bride's family) to see his daughters married. Bishop Nicholas heard of this dilemma and secretly dropped a bag of gold down their chimney. It landed in one of the girl's stockings, which had been hung out to dry. To this day, good boys and girls go to sleep on Christmas Eve hoping that they, too, will wake up to find their stockings filled on Christmas day.

Christmas Day

For many years my mom made the most incredible Christmas morning brunch for us. She served a Scandinavian pastry called a Maple Snowflake and a shrimp stir-fry prepared in a large skillet. The Maple Snowflake had to be made ahead of time and was not one of those quick and easy recipes. But she made it year after year because we loved it so much.

The menus, the events, and the special traditions have changed along with us. But one thing has never changed for me: Christmas is celebrated with family. This, the most important tradition, has been carried on year after year. (But that Maple Snowflake was delicious!)

Recipes from the kitchen of
Debbie's Mom, Ardis Kvare

MAPLE SNOWFLAKES

1 package (16 ounces) hot roll mix
1 cup hot water, 120°F to 130°F
1 egg
¾ cup granulated sugar, divided
6 tablespoons butter, melted and divided
3 teaspoons maple extract, divided
1½ teaspoons cinnamon
½ cup chopped pecans
1 can (16 ounces) vanilla frosting
Colored sugar (optional)

Combine roll mix and yeast packet in large bowl. Add hot water, egg,
¼ cup sugar, 2 tablespoons butter, and 1 teaspoon maple extract, stirring
until dough pulls away from sides of bowl. Knead on floured surface
5 minutes or until smooth. Cover dough with bowl; let stand 10 minutes.

Combine remaining ½ cup sugar, cinnamon, pecans, and 1 teaspoon
maple extract in small bowl; set aside. Grease two 12-inch pizza pans. Divide
dough into two equal pieces. Roll out one piece on lightly floured surface into
12-inch circle. Place onto prepared pan. Brush dough with 2 tablespoons melted
butter and sprinkle with ½ filling. Repeat with the other piece.

Make 1-inch circle in center of dough with cookie cutter or glass. Do not cut
through dough. Cut 16 wedges from outside edge just to circle. Twist each
wedge 5 times. Cover loosely; let rise 20 to 30 minutes or until doubled in size.

Preheat oven to 375°F. Bake twists 12 to 15 minutes or until lightly browned.
Combine frosting and remaining 1 teaspoon maple extract in small bowl.
Add small amount of water to make glaze. Place glaze in small plastic
food storage bag; cut off tiny corner of bag. Drizzle glaze over twists.
Sprinkle with colored sugar, if desired. Makes 2 twists or 32 servings.

From the kitchen of
Debbie's mom, Ardis Kvare

SHRIMP SCRAMBLE

9 large eggs
¼ cup milk or cream
½ teaspoon seasoned salt
½ teaspoon seasoned pepper
1¼ pounds medium shrimp, peeled and de-veined
4 tablespoons vegetable oil, divided
½ cup sliced celery
1 pound fresh bean sprouts
½ cup chopped green onions

Whisk together eggs, milk, seasoned salt, and pepper in large mixing bowl; set aside. Rinse shrimp with cold water; drain and pat dry with paper towels. Heat 2 tablespoons oil in large nonstick skillet over medium-high heat. Add shrimp; cook 3 to 4 minutes until pink and tender. Season to taste with additional seasoned salt and pepper. Remove shrimp and set aside.

Heat remaining 2 tablespoons oil in skillet. Add celery; cook 2 minutes. Stir in bean sprouts and onions. Cook 2 minutes; reduce heat to medium. Add reserved egg mixture and shrimp. Cook 4 minutes, stirring lightly until eggs are softly set. Reduce heat to low and serve immediately. Makes 6 servings.

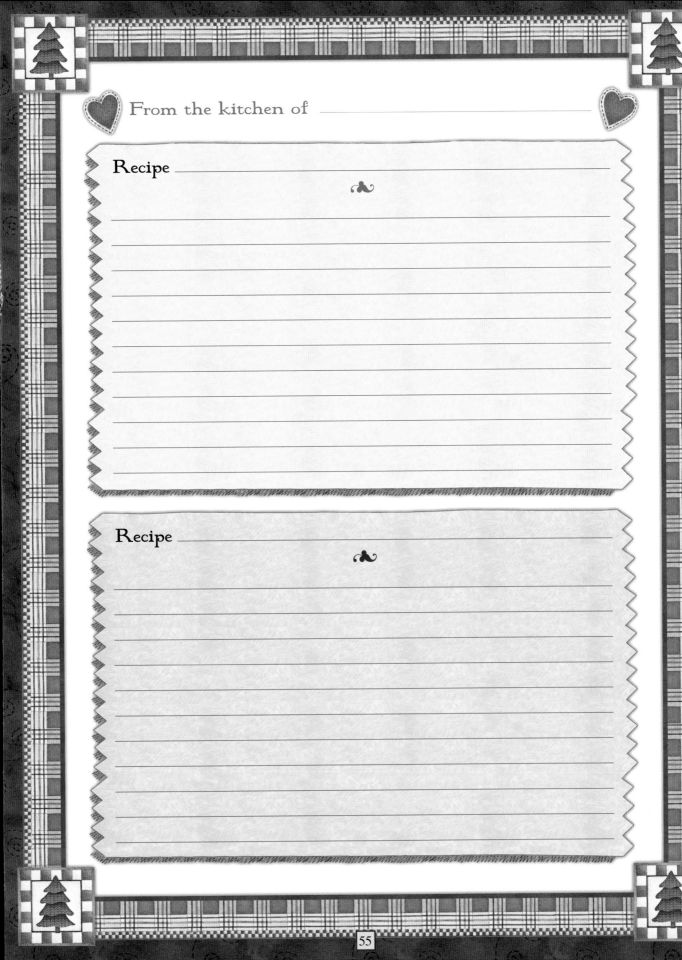

From the kitchen of _____

Recipe _____

Recipe _____

Christmas Memories

One of my favorite things about Christmas has always been the anticipation and preparation for the day. And when I was little, the anticipation often revolved around what was waiting under the tree. One year, my big dream was to have a dollhouse. My imagination was running wild when I saw the hugest present ever, wrapped up beautifully with my name on the gift tag. The photo at the front of this book captures the moment my dream came true.

I invite you to use the following pages to record your own special Christmas memories, and to display your favorite holiday photos. Make this keepsake a book you will enjoy for many years to come!

Our family Christmas dinner is usually at ....
....

The table is usually decorated with ....
....
....

Our traditional menu includes ....
....
....
....

When Christmas dinner is over ....
....
....

A favorite Christmas memory: ....
....
....
....
....
....
....
....
....
....
....
....
....

place
photo
here

place
photo
here

Thank You, Dear

I believe that the greatest joy in giving is to see how your gift lights up the face of its recipient. And if you've ever received a thank-you note, then you know how nice it is to feel your thoughts and efforts have been appreciated. Even though I'm busy, I always make a point of writing personal thank-you notes to each person who gives me a gift. The fact that it's less common to send letters will make them even more appreciated.

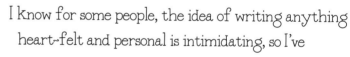

I know for some people, the idea of writing anything heart-felt and personal is intimidating, so I've provided you with a little guide to thank-you etiquette to get you started. Gather stickers and glitter for decorations and include your children in this process—it's a great way to instill some good old-fashioned manners and to make grandma and grandpa proud.

Thank-you note tips

❧

Always send a thank-you letter within a week of receiving a gift or being a guest in someone's home.

❧

Be sincere. Don't use words or expressions you wouldn't normally use.

❧

Include a personal anecdote that mentions the gift, what you like about it, and something about the gift-giver.

❧

Be proper. Use the example at right as a model for constructing your letter.

Here's an example:

December 29

Dear Aunt Clara,

Thank you so much for the beautiful sweater. I'm sure it will come in handy on our family vacation. You know how cold it gets at the cabin!

It was great seeing you, and I hope we can all get together again soon.

Love,
Susan

SPECIAL CASES

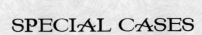

Monetary gifts

If a monetary gift was received, it is acceptable to say "Thank you for the money" or "Thank you for the check." It's also good to mention what plans you have for the gift.

Disliked gifts

If a gift is not particularly liked, try focusing on your gratitude for having received it. For example, "Thank you for the coffee mug. It will come in very handy for my morning coffee at work!"

Gifts to be returned

If a gift must be returned, there is no rule that says the gift-giver must be notified. Simply say thank you as graciously as possible for the gift that was given.